Laughter Effects:

Humor and Inspiration for Victims of

Sociopaths

by Andrea Irene Martin

Special contributor:
Lea Ross

"The greatest achievement was at first and for a time a dream. The oak sleeps in the acorn, the bird waits in the egg, and in the highest vision of the soul a waking angel stirs. Dreams are the seedlings of realities".

- *James Allen*

Table of Contents

A word of caution: *Laughter Effects: Humor ana Inspiration for Victims oj Sociopaths* is a support tool for your individual healing and should never be used to intentionally confront or banter with a sociopath. If you are in an abusive relationship, it's time to stop the violence. Call the National Domestic Violence Hotline at 1-800-799-SAFE (7233) or TTY 1-800-787-3224.

Impeccable Imposters

As we stare down on books with titles like *Snakes in Suits*, *In Sheep's Clothing*, *Emotional Vampires*, *Without Conscience*, *A Dance with the Devil*, and *The Sociopath Next Door*, conventional perceptions are stretched far beyond the comfort zone when we are forced to reckon with this cunning predator. Turning the pages in disbelief, we find sociopaths dwelling within the walls of our schools, workplaces, governments, churches, in the house next door, or right in our own bedroom. We marry them, have children with them, and sometimes even worship them.

1

Sociopaths are con "artists" with a talent for creating the perfect illusion, but their masterpieces inevitably evoke scenes more reminiscent of Dante's "Inferno" than Rembrandt's *Philosopher in Meditation*. They are opportunistic chameleons who project a captivating persona aimed at exploiting their victim's deepest hopes and dreams. When caught in a lie, they can wriggle out of it with the sort of panache that might have impressed escape artist Harry Houdini, and probably did. Throughout history, charismatic sociopaths have deceived individuals, groups, social systems, medical professionals, governments, and the legal system.

For most of us, the image that springs to mind is that of a serial killer, as portrayed in films by Stanley Kubrick or the twisted psychopath, Hannibal Lecter, in *Silence of the Lambs*. These films draw on actual case studies from the work of professionals like Robert Ressler, the FBI agent who coined the term "serial killer" in the 1970s (1), and Dr. Robert D. Hare, the developer of the Psychopathy Checklist (PCL). Dr. Hare's checklist is rooted in Hervey M. Cleckley's seminal work; *The Mask of Sanity*, originally published in 1941.

According to Dr. Robert Hare (*Without Conscience*) and Dr. Martha Stout (*The Sociopath Next Door*), sociopaths comprise between one and four percent of the population. Peering behind masks that still haunt detective files, we witness just a few of the victims that got caught in the tangled web and the predators that drew them in:

After watching a screening of the movie, *Precious*, actor/producer and screenwriter Tyler Perry wrote a letter to his fans, posted it on his website, and then revealed on Oprah that he had been sexually molested as a child. "Predators know when a child is vulnerable," Perry said. "And once they have you hooked, it's like being on a puppet-master's string; they keep you moving."

Statesman and Senator Scott Brown of Massachusetts revealed on an episode of "60 Minutes" and in his book, *Against All Odds* that he suffered sexual abuse as a child. He chillingly recalled how "Predators know when you are lost, and they can make you believe that no one will listen to you."

In the biggest game board on earth, "Wall Street," we witness sociopaths in tailored suits playing for different stakes, but nevertheless they descend upon their prey with the same lack of conscience. In the book, *13 Bankers*, by Simon Johnson and James Kwak, the authors noted a 1994 derivatives scandal that led to a lawsuit and criminal trial. They singled out the testimony of a derivatives salesman who gave what they called "the iconic quote of the era": "Lure people into that calm and then just totally fuck 'em". (2)

Another sociopath who acted out Oscar worthy performances on a world-wide stage is Christopher Rocancourt, the international jet-setting French con man, impostor, confidence man, and gentleman-thief

3

who scammed wealthy people by masquerading as a French member of the Rockefeller family. He convinced the rich, powerful, and Hollywood famous to invest forty million dollars in his schemes.

Rocancourt also married, fathered a child, and had an affair with another woman, and neither woman was aware of his con games or true identity. His elaborate network of flamboyant impersonations prompted the developer of the *Psychopathy Checklist*, Dr. Robert Hare, to muse, "I'd sure as hell like to have a close look at him". (3)

Barbara Bentley tells the story of her fourteen-year marriage to a person who convincingly portrayed himself as retired navy admiral, John Perry, in her book, *A Dance with the Devil*. When she first met him, he swept her off her feet with his intellectual and charming personality. As time went by, Barbara began to notice discrepancies in the stories he told about his previous professional life. While she struggled to put the pieces together, he drained her credit, dodged her questions, manipulated and misled her, and in the end tried to kill her.

In 2009, Barbara received the Paul H. Chapman Award in honor of her effort to change the divorce laws in California that allowed her abusive ex-husband to profit from his criminal behavior. Barbara received the award for making "positive influential differences in the United States criminal and civil justice arenas." The law

4

is available on Barbara's website:
www.adancewiththedevil.com.

   In addition to surviving her parents' painful divorce and the escalating abuse in their family home, Melissa G. Moore had to endure the unspeakable truth behind the man she called her father; she grew up with the gruesome serial killer known as the "Happy Face Killer." She was a teenager when her father was found guilty of killing eight women. She had to relearn what "normal" was through the observations of friends, outside family members, and peers. Through her ordeal, she became an advocate for the protection of victims of violence and the safety of children. She delivers a message of hope, healing, and empowerment in her memoir, *Shattered Silence: The Untold Story of a Serial Killer's Daughter*.
www.shatteredsilencebook.com

   In a real life story that is eerily reminiscent of *Tales from the Crypt*, Barbra Mastromarino had no idea that her husband was conducting illegal activity behind her back and that her perfect marriage would soon be shattered. On October 8, 2005, the U.S. Food and Drug Administration shut down her husband's human tissue recovery business, "Biomedical Tissue Services, Ltd."

   Dr. Michael Mastromarino and two other employees were convicted of illegally harvesting human bones, organs, tissue, and other cadaver parts from individuals awaiting cremation. With the help of funeral home directors, they forged numerous consent forms and then sold the illegally obtained body parts to medical companies without the consent of their families. Reports state that Dr. Mastromarino dissected more than 1,000 dead bodies over the years. He is now serving 18 to 54 years in prison for body stealing, forgery, grand larceny, and corruption. (4)

***

Psychologists compare the impact of the trauma from these experiences to the post-traumatic stress disorders that war veterans suffer. (5) We extend our gratitude to survivors who devote their time and experience to help other victims recover, and for leading the way out of the labyrinth.

Today, psychologists have new terms to describe sociopaths and psychopaths. Antisocial personality disorders twist and turn through the open weave nomenclature. The new terminology is as intricate as a spider's web and remains just as dangerous.

Antisocial Personality Disorder (ASPD or APD) is defined by the American Psychiatric Association's Diagnostic and Statistical Manual as "a pervasive pattern of disregard for, and violation of, the rights of others that begins in childhood or early adolescence and continues into adulthood." The World Health Organization's International Statistical Classification of Diseases and Related Health Problems defines a conceptually similar disorder as *Dissocial Personality Disorder,* though the two terms are not identical.

ASPD eventually replaced sociopathy as a diagnosis in the DSM. (6)

But the actual words "Antisocial Personality Disorder" fail to render the damage inflicted on victims by people that have no conscience. As my friend and fellow researcher Lea Ross describes it, "Those words are far too kind. They don't reflect the totality of the destruction or the years it takes victims to cut through the fog, if they ever do. Some victims go through life so traumatized they no longer have the trust to share their experience with anyone".

The search for answers and healing leads survivors through a maze that requires repeated navigation and spawns a journey that will ultimately challenge their mind, health, heart, and spirit.

Enter "Laughter Effects".

Laughter Effects: Humor and Inspiration for Victims of Sociopaths is a survivor's companion book of humor and inspiration designed to reduce the post-traumatic stress associated with exiting a relationship with a sociopath. Part inspirational, part educational and part comic book, the *Humor and Inspiration* section highlights more than sixty self-empowering comic images and reflections specifically created for people who have been victimized by a sociopath.

In addition, the *Navigating the Way Home* section lists a unique set of resources for survivors, including professionals who specialize in the positive effects of humor. The final section of *Laughter Effects* features a visual gallery of healing words and images designed to reduce the emotional stress associated with mental abuse.

Clinical studies confirm something mankind has relied on for stress relief since the dawn of civilization: "laughter is good medicine". Laughter reduces stress, strengthens the immune system, and benefits the cardiovascular system. (7) Laughter is a direct pathway to the center of one's identity. Humor is empowering! Physician and inspirational social activist Hunter "Patch" Adams is right when he says, "You treat a disease, you win or you lose. You treat a person I guarantee you'll win, no matter what the outcome." (8)

If you were victimized by a sociopath, it doesn't define who you are or limit the possibilities for a happy, healthy future. We have faith in the idea that laughter has the power to restore your spirit, your health and well being, and can help you move forward with life.

We hope to see you LAUGHING, LIVING, and DREAMING again.

Make humor part of the plan.

Enjoy.

Humor and Inspiration

"When humor goes, there goes civilization."

~ *Erma Bombeck*

"Laughter and tears are both responses to frustration and exhaustion. I myself prefer to laugh, since there is less cleaning up to do afterward."

~ Kurt Vonnegut

"Comedy is acting out optimism."

~ Robin Williams

"Never think you're better than anyone else, but don't let anyone treat you like you're worse than they are."

~ *Rip Torn*

"Comedy is very controlling - you are making people laugh."

~ *Gilda Radnor*

"Never let yesterday use up too much of today."

~ *Will Rogers*

"That's right, it's quitting time."

"I am thankful for laughter, except when milk comes out of my nose." ~ *Woody Allen*

"Acting deals with very delicate emotions. It is not putting up a mask. Each time an actor acts he does not hide; he exposes himself."

~ *Rodney Dangerfield*

Is a sociopath commanding your attention?
Take a quiet moment to visualize a few of the
following words and images:

"Take a number please"......
You are # 1,925,439.

"As you can see, I don't have time for games."

"Don't you think I've carried you long enough?"

"Please make an appointment with my secretary (if he feels like answering the phone, he'll be happy to assist you)."

"Would you like to be placed on the waiting list? You better hurry, they're just wrapping it up."

"On second thought, I don't think you're as bad as people say……..

……..you're worse."

"Would you like fries with that order?"

"I'd like to help you out.
Now which way did you come in?"

"I'll always cherish the initial misconceptions I had about you."

"I'm so glad I bought that aniti-BS software."

"Let me put my reply in language that you can understand."

"I'm busy now, can I ignore you some other time?"

"Yes, as a matter of fact I do keep your correspondence on file."

"Maybe this will help you.......? It's available at the drug store without a prescription."

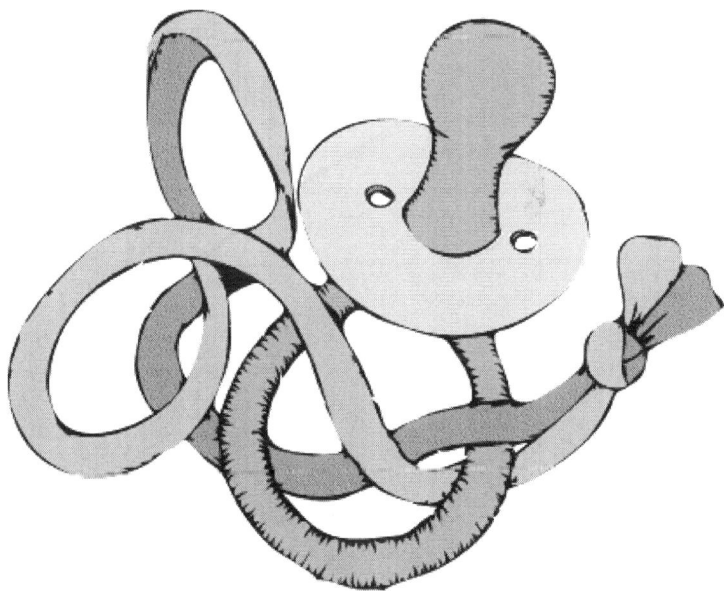

25

"Who did you say you were?"

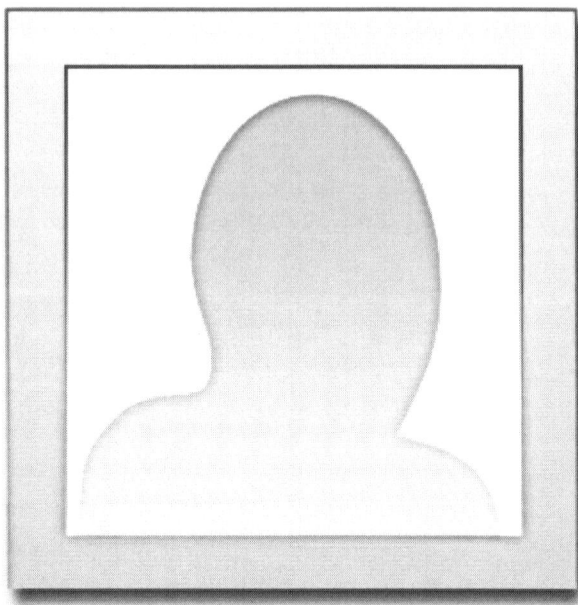

"Don't blame yourself; let me do that."

"Did hell freeze over already? That was quick."

"Deja Moo; this BS looks familiar."

"Weren't you voted off the planet?"

"I thought so. Beam him up Scotty."

"When are you going to use the Miss Manners Gift Certificate I bought for you? I'm still waiting."

"People said you were amazing. Now I understand what they meant…….."

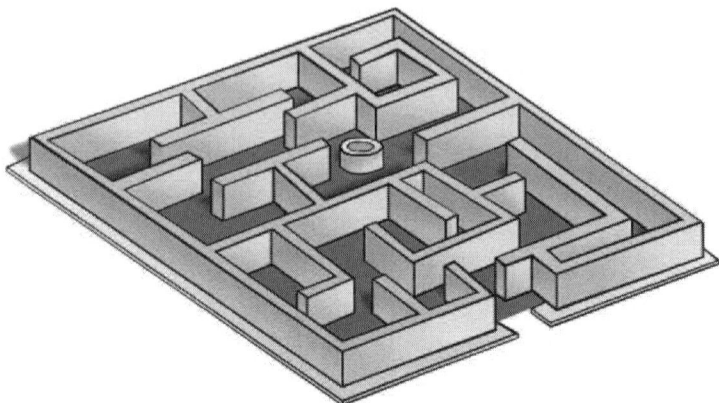

"Thanks for thinking of me, but I'm going to skip this one."

We added the following images and a touch of humor to a few sociopath character traits:

Pathological Lying:

Go with your instincts and do your homework. If it doesn't walk like a duck or quack like a duck, then it's probably not a duck.

Superficial Charm:

Don't be deceived by superficial charm.

Ask questions.

Grandiosity:

Investigate "sparkling" accounts of accomplishments and a grandiose sense of self worth. Their claims should be backed up by facts. If it sounds too good to be true, it probably isn't.

Sociopaths are manipulative. Do not allow
anyone to direct the show at your expense.

HELL THEATRE

Sociopaths may display a lack of remorse or guilt when transgressions occur. Trust your human instincts.

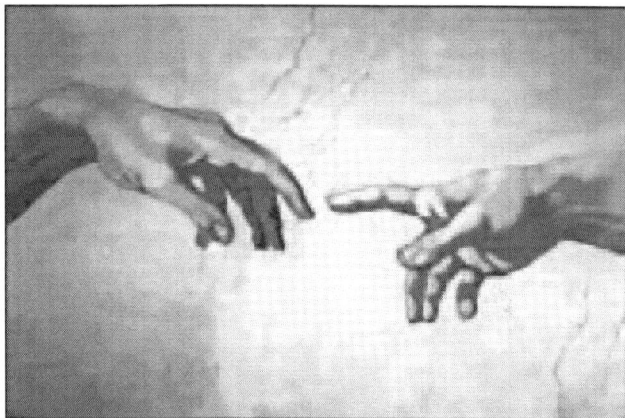

Sociopaths don't take responsibility for their own actions. They believe the rules don't apply to them. You are not responsible for their actions.

Be on the lookout for callousness or lack of empathy.

Don't make excuses for their behavior.

Sociopaths lack realistic long term goals.

Sociopaths can be versatile at criminal activity.

Do not play their game or try to get even.

Don't role the dice.

Check out – not checkmate.

Observe the "no contact" rule whenever possible.

And most of all.......LIVE WELL.

NAVIGATING THE WAY HOME

Robert Hare:

If we designed a road map to guide us through the maze of information about sociopaths, psychopaths, and antisocial personality disorders, the first signpost on the journey would point the way to Dr. Robert Hare. Dr. Hare is a psychologist who devoted most of his academic career to the investigation of psychopathy, its nature, assessment, and implications for mental health and criminal justice. Demonstrating integrity, he never participates in the sensationalism that often surrounds revelations about psychopaths. (9) He remains steadfast in his commitment to define the dynamics behind the mask.

Dr. Hare is the author of several books, including one of the definitive works on psychopathy, *Without a Conscience: The Disturbing World of the Psychopaths Among Us.* He developed the current standard for identifying psychopaths, "The Psychopathy Checklist-Revised" (PCL-R). Prior to the development of the PCL-R, the international research community of psychologists and clinical professionals lacked a standard measure. The "Hare Psychopathy Checklist" is an excellent resource for distinguishing the difference between sociopaths and psychopaths.

Dr. Hare is Emeritus Professor of Psychology at the University of British Columbia, where he has taught and conducted research for more than four decades. In addition, he is President of Darkstone Research Group

Ltd., a forensic research and consulting firm. He consults with law enforcement agencies, including the FBI and the RCMP, sits on the Research Advisory Board of the new FBI Child Abduction and Serial Murder Investigative Resources Center (CASMIRC), and is a member of the FBI Serial Murder Working Group.

Please visit Dr. Hare's website for an in-depth biography of his life and other valuable resources for survivors at: www.hare.org.

We also recommend Robert Hercz's article, *Psychopaths Among Us* for an informative overview of Dr. Hare's career. Originally published in an online issue of *Saturday Night Magazine*, it is available on Dr. Hare's web site: http://www.hare.org/links/saturday.html.

In addition, there is a free excerpt from *Without a Conscience* available at the online journal, *Psychology Today*, entitled, "This Charming Psychopath; How to spot social predators before they attack," by Robert Hare, published on January 01, 1994 - last reviewed on June 01, 2010: http://www.psychologytoday.com/articles/199401/charming-psychopath

Dr. Hare devotes much of his time and expertise to *Aftermath: Surviving Psychopathy*, an organization dedicated to educating the public regarding the nature of psychopathy and its cost to individuals and society. The Aftermath organization supports research that aims to: prevent or minimize the development of psychopathic

46

traits, reduce the impact of psychopathic traits, and understand and treat the aftermath of psychopathy. Its primary goal is to reduce the negative impact of psychopathy on families and victims of psychopathic individuals.

"From the beginning, *Aftermath: Surviving Psychopathy* has been dedicated to all who seek to understand this personality disorder and the toll it takes on those whose lives intersect with the affected. After many months of weekly conference calls and many email exchanges, the website was launched in April of 2008. Our working group has grown larger as other researchers, therapists and survivors have joined."

The Aftermath website is the best source for a free Scribed edition of Harvey Cleckley's, *The Mask of Sanity*:

www.aftermath-surviving-psychopathy.org
http://www.scribd.com/doc/4715591/Cleckley-The-Mask-of-Sanity

Aftermath has an active forum and many useful resource links, including *Bully Online*, (a project of the Tim Field Foundation) and Lovefraud.com.

Robert Hare is affiliated with Dr. Paul Babiak, an industrial and organizational psychologist with over thirty years of experience coaching executives and managers on a variety of people-related issues in the workplace. Babiak and Hare extended the theory and research on psychopathy to the business and corporate world, with the development of the B-Scan-360, a 360° instrument used to screen for psychopathic traits and behaviors (10), and a book, *Snakes in Suits: When Psychopaths Go To Work*.

We also recommend the five part documentary *Psychopath – Psychopath*. Dr. Hare and his peers take viewers behind state penitentiary walls for an unnerving look inside the minds of criminal psychopaths, and they delve into the latest research. The entire series is available on youtube and has a run-time of about fifty minutes. Part one: http://www.youtube.com/watch?v=2PaQjV_onl0

Martha Stout:

Traveling further down the road to the next signpost on the map, we face another sociopath living right next door or just around the corner. This is the sociopath unfettered by prison walls or workplace rules. In her book *The Sociopath Next Door*, Dr. Martha Stout states "The only difference between sociopathy and criminality is whether or not they get caught." (11)

Martha Stout, Ph.D. is an American psychologist and author of several books on the subject of sociopathy. She completed her professional training in psychology at the McLean Psychiatric Hospital. She served as an instructor on the faculty of the Harvard Medical School for over twenty-five years and served as part of the graduate faculty of The New School, the Massachusetts School of Professional Psychology, and Wellesley College. (12)

Dr. Stout's case studies shed light on people's vulnerabilities, especially those with a trusting nature. Sociopaths excel at using logic to distort the truth and alter reality. They knock us off balance emotionally and psychologically to gain the advantage over us. Dr. Stout advises developing an awareness of the nature of anti-social behavior in order to avoid becoming a victim. She proposes thirteen rules as self-help guidelines to assess relationships and certain behavioral characteristics, as well as offering advice on handling situations when one encounters the behavior.

Martha Stout's list of *Thirteen Rules for Dealing with Sociopaths in Everyday Life* is widely available online, but I recommend reading her book. It is a real eye-opener about what people are capable of doing (and getting away with), even in their own families.

Sandra L. Brown:

Sandra L. Brown, M.A. is a psychopathologist and CEO of The Institute for Relational Harm Reduction & Public Psychopathy Education. Her books include *Women Who Love Psychopaths, How to Spot a Dangerous Man Before You Get Involved*, and *Counseling Victims of Violence: A Handbook for Helping Professionals*.

49

Ms. Brown is recognized for her pioneering work on women's issues related to relational harm with Cluster B/Axis II/Sociopathy/Pyschopathy disordered partners. She specializes in the development of Pathological Love Relationship clinical training and survivor support services. Her organization is not a non-profit, but her website provides many useful, free articles and resources for learning how to protect yourself.

www.saferelationshipsmagazine.com

Unmasking Sexual Con Games:

We recommend *Unmasking Sexual Con Games* by Kathleen M. McGee and Laura J. Buddenberg, specifically for the insight in Chapter Seven, "The Many Masks of the Emotional Groomer." This book is a leader's guide to help teens avoid emotional grooming and dating violence, but the guidelines can be applied to victims across the board, regardless of age.

In Chapter Seven, students participated in a classroom project that illustrated how they felt about their involvement in sexual con games. The students (both girls and boys) made masks out of papier mache or plaster and painted them to express certain feelings and emotions. They wrote about what the masks meant. They describe the pain they have caused in others or have felt themselves. Their stories are real. Some of these students were targets, and some were sexual con artists. *Unmasking Sexual Con Games* is available through online retailers, and Chapter Seven can be viewed at "Google Books Unmasking Sexual Con Games."

Clinical study: for readers interested in expanding their knowledge of clinical psychopathy:

"The Society for the Scientific Study of Psychopathy" (SSSP) is a non-profit, professional organization that promotes the conduct and communication of scientific research in the field of psychopathy, and encourages education and training in those fields of science that contribute to research in psychopathy.
www.psychopathysociety.org

Laura Kamienski:

Laura Kamienski is the former director of "Kicks Martial Arts for Women" in Lewisburg, Pennsylvania, and the creator of "Empower! Self-Defense for Women." The following excerpt is available on her blog:

"It can happen to anyone…NPD unmasked."

"For the past decade I have taught women and girls to protect themselves. I am considered an expert in the field of women's self-defense. My course consists not only of helping women to learn to protect their bodies, but includes activities designed to help women develop skills to protect their hearts as well.

Over the last few months I've been asking myself

51

how it happened that in 2007-2008 I found myself immersed in an emotionally abusive relationship to the point of losing my heart, soul and all of my self-esteem. A relationship that robbed me of my essence and destroyed my capacity to believe in the goodness of humanity. The answer is that I fell in love with a man with……Narcissistic Personality Disorder."
- Laura Kamienski 11/23/2008

Laura has evolved beyond the bonds of victimization and "found peace" as she says in her last blog entry dated September 2010, but her blog remains intact as an educational digital journal of hope and recovery for survivors of narcissistic abuse. (update; as of this writing, Laura has added a new post in May of 2011 "Resurfacing Hope"). http://laurakamienski.blogspot.com

After seven years, the Kicks Martial Arts Center closed its doors in 2008 as Laura followed her dream to Tucson, Arizona. Congratulations Laura! The following excerpt is from the portion of the Kicks Martial Arts Center website entitled 'Empower ! Self Defense for Women': www.kicks4women.com.

"The reality that women are usually assaulted by a known assailant means that self-defense skills for women should primarily include learning skills to recognize and defend against assaults committed by a trusted friend, neighbor or intimate partner. In other words, classes should begin to account for the emotional and psychological dynamics of the common relationships between victim and perpetrator. Some martial artists teaching self-defense for women, even while acknowledging that assailants are typically not strangers, tend to ignore the relationships and emotional dynamics that exist between victim and perpetrator."

Ms. Kamienski was a regular guest speaker and instructor at various institutions, including Susquehanna, Bucknell and Syracuse Universities. She has written numerous articles about women and the martial arts for a variety of publications. Her awards include World Wide Black Belt Hall of Fame Woman of the Year 2002 and Instructor of the Year 2001. (13)

She also co-authored a book with Jennifer Lawler, entitled, *Training Women in the Martial Arts: A Special Journey*. The authors highlight everyday interactions with families, friends, coworkers, students, bosses, and others who may attempt to keep us in gender role boxes. They provide advice on how to recognize these interactions and counteract them. Laura's personal website is: www.kamienski.net

Gift From Within:

"Gift From Within" is an International public charity organization for survivors of trauma and victimization. This organization is an essential resource guide for both survivors and caregivers of Post Traumatic Stress Disorder. Their website offers training and expertise to people who suffer from PTSD, those at risk for PTSD, and those who care for traumatized individuals.

"Gift From Within" develops and disseminates educational material, including videotapes, articles, books, and other materials, through their website, and they maintain a roster of survivors who are willing to participate in an international network of peer support.

They also have an excellent Support Pal network that contributes to a wide range of issues including inspiration, healing, living with PTSD, humor, book reviews, favorite books and movies, and finding a therapist. I found the Support Pal stories and information encouraging and inspiring. The web address to the "Support Pals Humor Grab Bag" is: www.giftfromwithin.org/html/humor.html www.giftfromwithin.org.

The National Domestic Violence Hotline:

"The National Domestic Violence Hotline" was established in 1996 as a component of the Violence Against Women Act (VAWA), passed by Congress. The Hotline is a nonprofit organization that provides crisis intervention, information and referral to victims of domestic violence, perpetrators, friends and families. The Hotline answers a variety of calls and is a resource for domestic violence advocates, government officials, law enforcement agencies and the general public. The Hotline serves as the only domestic violence hotline in the nation with access to more than 4,000 shelters and domestic violence programs across the United States, Puerto Rico and the U.S. Virgin Islands. Advocates receive approximately 23,500 calls each month.

The Hotline is toll-free, confidential and anonymous. It operates 24 hours a day, 365 days a year, in more than 170 different languages through interpreter services, with a TTY line available for the Deaf, Deaf-Blind and Hard of Hearing. The staff at the Hotline is also available to provide assistance and guidance in a variety of areas, including media, public relations, fundraising, public policy, legal advocacy and public education and training. If you are in an abusive relationship, it's time to stop the violence. Call the National Domestic Violence Hotline at 1-800-799-SAFE (7233) or TTY 1-800-787-3224. www.thehotline.org

The National Center for Victims of Crime:

The "National Center for Victims of Crime" is the nation's leading resource and advocacy organization for crime victims and those who serve them. Since its inception in 1985, the National Center has worked with grassroots organizations and criminal justice agencies throughout the United States serving millions of crime victims. The mission of the National Center for Victims of Crime is to forge a national commitment to help victims of crime rebuild their lives. They are dedicated to serving individuals, families, and communities harmed by crime.

Please consult the NCVC Resource Center for important information about Dating Violence, Stalking and Victim Law. Additional legislation was passed due to the inspiring efforts of victims and their friends and family. Be sure to visit their "Helpful Contacts" section that includes many free hot lines for victims of abuse and other crimes. www.ncvc.org

LAUGHTER IS GOOD MEDICINE:

Patch Adams and the Gesundheit! Institute.

Hunter Doherty "Patch" Adams, M.D. is an American physician, citizen diplomat and author. He is well-known for his work as a medical doctor and a clown, but he is also a social activist who has devoted 40 years to changing America's health care system.

He believes that laughter, joy and creativity are an integral part of the healing process. His life inspired the movie *Patch Adams*, starring Robin Williams. In collaboration with the institute based in Arlington, Virginia, Dr. Adams promotes a different health care model (one not funded by insurance policies). (14)

Founded in 1971, The Gesundheit! Institute is a project in holistic medical care based on the belief that one cannot separate the health of the individual from the health of the family, the community, the world, and the health care system itself.

A subscription to Funny Times Magazine costs $25; 100% of subscription dollars go to help build the "Patch Adams Teaching Center and Clinic." There is also a free weekly email, "Take a Break Cartoon," and access to the archive from previous weeks.

www.patchadams.org - www.funnytimes.com

The Humor Project:

"Making the world happier one smile at a time."

Founded by Dr. Joel Goodman in 1977, "The HUMOR Project, Inc." is an organization that focuses on the positive power of humor. The project has provided grants to 450+ schools, hospitals, and human service agencies to help them develop services and resources that tap the positive power of humor.

Dr. Goodman is the author of eight best-selling books and the former editor of *Laughing Matters* magazine. He also founded "AHA!, The American Humor Association", which includes over 165,000 humor conspirators. He believes that it is essential for business to "do well and do good" at the same time.

Dr. Goodman takes his work seriously, and he takes himself lightly as he helps people to get more "smileage" out of their lives and jobs. His book, *Laffirmations: 1,001 Ways to Add Humor to Your Life and Work*, is a rich collection of quotations to strengthen your sense of humor. Each day of the year includes a thought-provoking quotation or question designed to help readers discover where humor already exists in their lives, and where they need to add a dash. It includes quotes by *Bill Cosby, Lily Tomlin, Jerry Seinfeld* and many other humorists.

www.humorproject.com

Laughter Yoga: Dr. Madan Kataria:

Laughter Yoga International is a "Global Movement for Health, Joy and World Peace." The following information from the Laughter Yoga website explains what Laughter Yoga is: "Laughter Yoga is a revolutionary idea – simple and profound. It is an exercise routine and complete wellbeing workout. Laughter Yoga combines Unconditional Laughter with Yogic Breathing (Pranayama)." Dr. Madan Kataria has been promoting the benefits of laughter since 1995.

Dr. Kataria explains that anyone can "laugh for no reason" without relying on humor, jokes or comedy. Laughter Yoga groups simulate laughter with a body exercise using eye contact and childlike playfulness, and it soon turns into real and contagious laughter. The concept of Laughter Yoga is based on the scientific fact that the body cannot differentiate between fake and real laughter; either one offers the same physiological and psychological benefits.

"My goal is to have one million laughter clubs around the world within the next ten years," said Dr. Madan Kataria at Pangea Day 2008 as he addressed millions of people via satellite on Saturday from Stage 15 at Sony Studios. (Pangea Day is a global initiative for world peace that unites people worldwide through the power of cinema). He and actress Goldie Hawn led the audience in several moments of roaring laughter across the planet.

Clinical research on Laughter Yoga methods conducted at the University of Graz in Austria; Bangalore, India and in the United States proved that laughter lowers the level of stress hormones (epinephrine, cortisol, etc) in the blood. It fosters a positive and hopeful attitude. It is less likely for a person to succumb to stress and feelings of depression and helplessness if they can laugh away their troubles.

Laughter Yoga Clubs are free, non-political, non-religious, non-profit and run directly by *Laughter Clubs International* in India and *Laughter Yoga International* in the rest of the world. There are no membership fees, no forms to fill out, and no fuss. The Clubs are operated by Laughter Yoga Leaders and volunteers trained as Laughter Yoga Teachers. Please see Dr. Kataria's website for his "Ten Good Reasons to Laugh for No Reason", and for more information about how to participate: www.laughteryoga.org

In 2001, Dr. Kataria introduced actor and comedian

of "Monty Python" fame *John Cleese* to Laughter Yoga when they traveled to Mumbai together to film the four-part BBC TV mini-series, *The Human Face*. Dr. Kataria took John to a Laughter Club and a prison where they laughed with the inmates. During a four-minute youtube video entitled *Benefits of Laughter Yoga with John Cleese*, Cleese states, "I was struck by how laughter CONNECTS you with people. It's almost impossible to maintain any kind of distance or any sense of social hierarchy when you're just howling with laughter. Laughter is a force for democracy."

In conclusion:

We observed a complete opposite – a total eclipse - to the interconnectedness of laughter in the following words by Dr. Tom Powel, head of the therapy program at the Vermont State Penitentiary. During an interview with an inmate in the documentary *Psychopath – Psychopath*, Dr. Powel remarked, "If one looks beyond the words and gauges the effect of the emotion, the feeling that goes with the words, at that point you start to see a DISCONNECT with what he is saying and what he is experiencing."

People that get involved in a relationship with a sociopath can sense this disconnect. Follow your instincts, do your homework, question their motives, and seek out other opinions. Along the way, we discovered that humor can reduce the impact of the post-traumatic stress associated with exiting a relationship with a sociopath. Laughter isn't a cure but rather a coping mechanism that provides us with a new perspective. As Laughter Therapist Enda Junkins says, "It changes the way you relate to the situation." (15) We hope it does the same for you.

Andrea Irene Martin and *Lea Ross* can be contacted at:

andreairenemartin@gmail.com

LOVE

Psychological abuse can send victims into a state of deep despair. The following words and images are specifically focused on healing from emotional trauma.

PEACE

CONNECTEDNESS

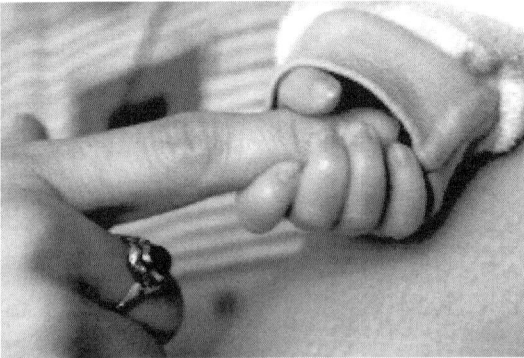

HARMONY

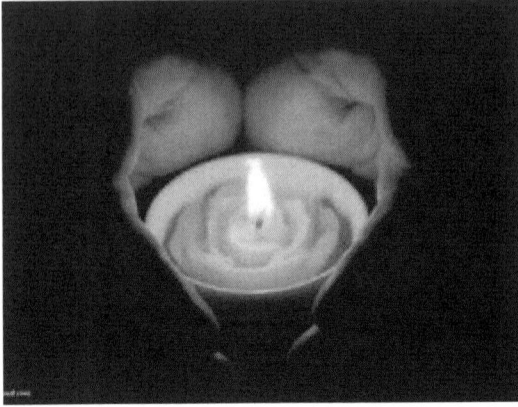

RECEPTIVITY

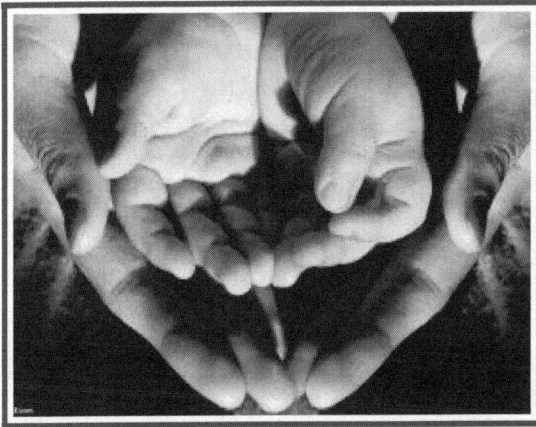

ESSENCE

GENTLENESS

COMMUNICATION

ENTHUSIASM

TENDERNESS

BEAUTY

TRANQUILITY

PERSPECTIVE

CONTEMPLATION

CONTENTMENT

BLISS

HAPPINESS

SHARING

POSSIBILITIES

DISCOVERY

CONSCIOUSNESS

GROWTH

IMAGINATION

CONGRATULATIONS!

You made it to the BEGINNING…..

(Did you see the Hummingbird in the photos?)

Our friend 'No Toe': the bird with a conscience.

A dear old bird...
'No Toe'.

A bird without a toe
Often comes to visit me
We talk a lot in riddles
Like antennae in a tree
However he does vocalize
The things I cannot see
His sulphur crested vision
Ruffled for a fee
Dreaming with this
cockatoo
I laugh and do agree
He really has a conscience
Gracious like a bee
The enigmatic puzzle here
Full circle back to zee
Conditional exclamation
marks
After golly, gosh and gee!!!

Readers Journal
Express yourself.

ME WORRY?

Readers Journal
Add your own images.

Readers Journal

Readers Journal

Bayon Temple at Angkor, Cambodia. (16)

Notes:

1. Former FBI agent, Robert K. Ressler.
   http://en.wikipedia.org/wiki/Robert_Ressler

2. *The Thirteen Bankers* by Simon Johnson and James Kwak, Pantheon Books, NY; pg 8.

3. *Psychopaths Among Us* by Robert Hercz is available at www.hare.org link media articles.
   http://www.hare.org/links/saturday.html

4. "Dentist Pleads Guilty to Stealing and Selling Body Parts" by Alan Feuer: The New York Times, March 19, 2008.
   http://www.nytimes.com/2008/03/19/nyregion/thecity/19bones.html

5. "Still Having Nightmares About My Sociopathic Ex".
   http://counsellingresource.com/ask-the-psychologist/2009/08/31/nightmares-about-my-sociopathic-ex/

6. Antisocial Personality Disorder - Diagnostic and Statistical Manual of Mental Disorders Fourth edition Text Revision (DSM-IV-TR) American Psychiatric Association (2000) - pages 645–650.
   http://en.wikipedia.org/wiki/Antisocial_personality_disorder

7. *Is Laughter the Best Medicine?* by Carol Sowell; MDA Publications (Muscular Dystrophy Association) Vol. 3 No 4 1996.
   http://www.mdausa.org/publications/Quest/q34laughter.html

8. Dr. Hunter "Patch" Adams quotation:
   http://en.wikiquote.org/wiki/Patch_Adams_(film)

9. *Psychopaths Among Us* by Robert Hercz.

10. *Psychopathic C.E.O.'s* by Michael Steinberger; New York Times Magazine, Dec. 12, 2004.
http://www.nytimes.com/2004/12/12/magazine/12PSYCHO.html

11. *The Sociopath Next Door* by Martha Stout, Broadway Books, NY; pg. 81

12. American Psychologist, Dr. Martha Stout:
http://en.wikipedia.org/wiki/Martha_Stout

13. Laura Kamienski: 2001 Tae Kwon Do Instructor of the Year, 2002 World Karate Union Instructor of the Year.
http://www.kicks4women.com/instructors.shtml

14. Biography; Dr. Hunter Doherty "Patch" Adams.
http://en.wikipedia.org/wiki/Patch_Adams

15. *The Role of Laughter in Psychotherapy* by Laughter Therapist Enda Junkins. www.laughtertherapy.com

16. Bayon Temple, Angkor Cambodia.
http://en.wikipedia.org/wiki/Bayon

Credits:

Clip art images courtesy of www.WPClipart.com and www.PDClipart.com.

Bayon Temple images at Angkor, Cambodia courtesy of Justin Watt: www.junstinsomnia.org

"Felix the Cat" image and other Wikipedia sources: Creative Commons Attribution License.

Photos: courtesy of Sam Mugraby at www.photos8.com, and individual contributors at morgueFile. www.morguefile.com.

"No Toe" images and poetry lovingly donated by a friend.

Cover created by Andrea I. Martin (mask image courtesy of patricia-fortes at morgueFile.com).

A special thanks to my co-contributor Lea Ross for her "absolutely fabulous" sense of humor, and everyone who volunteered their time and experience to make this book possible.

Through personal experience, we learned that laughter can help us to move forward in life with a new perspective. We hope it does the same for you.

- *Andrea I. Martin & Lea Ross*

"I'm so glad I bought that aniti-BS software."

From *Feathered Quill Book Reviews*:

"For most everyone, Antisocial Personality Disorder (Sociopaths) brings to mind haunting movie characters like Hannibal Lecter from *Silence of the Lambs*. But the author of this book, with contributions from a co-author, references real cases as well as how the term "serial killer" was coined by an FBI agent in the 1970's, named Robert Ressler. But APD goes a whole lot further than a character in a movie. In fact, current research estimates that the number of people afflicted with APD is somewhere between 1 in 25 and 1 in 100. No, that does not mean Hannibal Lecter's are walking the planet – it means that there are those who suffer from a disorder that most likely came from having a life where they were abused or harmed in some manner on a daily basis.

To deceive the world is the main goal of a sociopath. Whether a sociopath deceives victims, doctors, bosses - they are predators who usually draw crowds because the crowd sees them as someone with courage, determination, and power. AND, oddly enough, they believe what these sociopaths are saying (think Hitler on his dais).

It seems strange to insert "Laugher is the best medicine," at this point, but it is true. We use humorous words and images as a defense mechanism; they help neutralize the negative impacts of Post Traumatic Stress and allow the mind and body to calm down. Humor is also a form of empowerment; the ability to laugh overrides the anger, decreases stress, bolsters the immune system, and helps the cardio vascular system all at the same time.

This incredible little book not only shows readers various words and images of humor that can help with the effects of APD, but it also gives a guide of internet sties, organizations, books, research, and contributions from a variety of doctors (i.e., Patch Adams) and the work they do to help others.

Although this is quite a small book, it holds a great deal of punch. It explores the world of the sociopath - the ever-changing chameleon - and gives the research and humor necessary to begin helping others in the world of psychopathy, sociopathy, and psychology."

Quill Says: "A remarkable look at a world that is something we would all rather not see, but should know ahead of time how to deal with."